SOUNDS
OF THE
SAVANNA

To Jacob,
Read & roar!

Terry Catasús Jennings

by Terry Catasús Jennings   illustrated by Phyllis Saroff

Dawn kisses the grasslands of the savanna. A lion roars. Long vocal cords vibrate in his throat—back and forth, back and forth. The cords make the air around them move. When one molecule of air moves, its neighbor moves—back and forth, back and forth. The sound of the lion's roar spreads out in waves. It ripples like a pebble dropped into the water.

The roar lets other lions of his pride know where he is. It warns strangers away from his territory.

From a lake miles away, a lioness responds. Her answer carries over the water. It's still early and the sound travels clearly. A herd of wildebeests hears the roar from across the lake. It sounds as if the lioness is next to them.

The wildebeests know the lioness isn't hunting. Predators hunt quietly. But since the roar seems so close, wildebeest males sound the alarm with low-pitched bellows. Parents surround their babies. The wildebeests run back and forth quickly on the opposite shore. *See?* They seem to say to the lioness, *we're all healthy and fast. We will outrun you. Don't waste your energy on us.* The tramping of their hooves is loud. The lioness hears it.

The sun rises on the savanna. Elephants at a watering hole sense danger. They herd their babies tight and trumpet. Their sounds are loud— full of energy—and high-pitched. They also rumble low-pitched sounds that travel far, very far. Other elephants can pick up the rumbles from miles away. Most other animals can't hear them, even if they're close.

The mid-morning sun warms the savanna. Vervet monkeys skitter through the grassland. Along the way, they eat figs, leaves, seeds, flowers, eggs, insects and, occasionally, young chicks. They store seeds and nuts in their cheek pouches for later. Last night, the troop slept in trees bordering the savanna. Tonight they'll return, but for now they enjoy their time in the grassland.

One vervet monkey spies an eagle.

K-kawh, he yells. His call is loud so the rest of his troop can hear him. They hide in low-lying bushes and brush. The eagle goes away hungry.

K-cheu! Another alarm. A different sound but just as loud. Several monkeys gang up on a snake. The troop gets away from another predator.

The noon sun beats down on the savanna. Baboons have come down from the rocky cliffs to the grassland. They feed. They eat roots, grasses, insects, birds' eggs, and small vertebrates. They sometimes even eat baby baboons.

A little baboon drifts away from her mother. A hungry male baboon visiting the troop sees her and follows.

In the stranger's hands, the young baboon shrieks. Her high-pitched cry alerts her own troop to come to the rescue. Soon the baby is with her mother once again. The baboons rest. They groom each other. The sound of soft, low-pitched grunts drifts from the troop. All safe.

The mid-afternoon sun bakes the savanna. Thirsty zebras drink by the water's edge. A familiar smell fills the still air—a frightening scent.

Heeaw, heeaw, heeaw! A zebra sounds a loud, high-pitched alarm.

The herd runs. Will they be able to protect their babies from the leopard?

The sun sets on the savanna. Spiny mice scurry through the golden grass looking for a meal.

An owl has the same idea. She swoops between the grasses and grabs one of the tiny mice in her talons. A high-pitched squeal escapes from the spiny mouse's tiny throat. The rest of the mice scatter, quivering with fright.

But the owl's idea doesn't work. The mouse's brittle skin tears off. When the owl lifts, the tiny mouse drops to the ground. Only a scaly patch of skin hangs from the owls' deadly talons. The spiny mouse is safe. Tomorrow, his skin will start to grow back, hair and all.

Night has fallen on the savanna. Hunters are on the prowl. A yellow-winged bat flies away from her roost, looking for prey. Her baby hangs from her, learning to hunt. The bat makes very high-pitched sounds. Other bats can hear the pinging noises. Some insects that bats like to eat can also hear them. Most animals hear nothing.

When the sound waves hit something hard, they bounce back. The echoes reach the bats' big ears and lead them to their prey.

After a night of hunting, the bat and her baby return to the roost with full tummies.

The moon rises over the savanna. A lioness stalks. Not a peep comes from her throat. She makes not a sound, padding quietly, hidden by the tall grass. She surprises a herd of gazelles. In one pounce, she has food for her babies.

The soft purrs from her den greet her ears when she nears.

The lion cubs eat. They stretch.
It's quiet time in the savanna.

For Creative Minds

Sound Waves

Sound starts with movement. A molecule vibrates—it moves quickly back and forth. It bumps the molecule next to it and sets it vibrating. Molecules of air around them move. The vibration spreads away from the starting point in waves, like when you drop a pebble in water.

Inside ears are tiny hairs, too small to see without a microscope. When a sound wave touches them, they vibrate. The brain understands the vibration as sound.

As the sound moves out from its starting point, the vibrations make a wave pattern. Waves have two characteristics: amplitude and frequency.

Amplitude is the height of a wave. In sound waves, this is the **volume**. Volume tells how much vibrational energy is in a sound. High-volume sounds are loud. Low-volume sounds are quiet.

Frequency is the distance from the top (peak) of one wave to the top of the next wave. This is a sound's **pitch**. High-pitched sound is made when the particles vibrate very quickly and the waves are close together. Low-pitched sound is made when the particles move more slowly and the waves are spaced out.

All sound has both characteristics: high or low pitch and high or low volume. Look at these sound waves and think of the animals that make them.

What kinds of sound can you make?

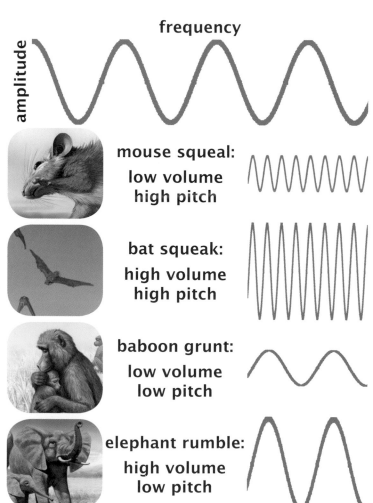

frequency

amplitude

mouse squeal:
low volume
high pitch

bat squeak:
high volume
high pitch

baboon grunt:
low volume
low pitch

elephant rumble:
high volume
low pitch

Sound Experiments

Touch Vibrations

Talk or sing a song. Hold your hand in front of your mouth. Do you feel any movement or vibrations in the air? While you are talking or singing, use your fingertip to touch your cheeks, lips, tongue, teeth, throat, and collarbone.

Can you tell where the vibration is the strongest? That is where your sound starts!

Many animals, including humans, have vocal cords (vocal folds) inside the voice box (larynx), which is inside the throat. When you talk or sing, you push air up from your lungs. The air travels over the vocal cords. The muscles in the larynx move the vocal cords to control the pitch and volume of your sound.

Make Vibrations

For this experiment you will need:
- a piece of cardboard at least six inches across
- scissors
- rubber bands of different sizes: small and big, thick and thin
- a pencil

Cut a hole about three inches wide in your piece of cardboard. Wrap several rubber bands around the cardboard. Slide the pencil under the rubber bands to create a "bridge" that holds the rubber bands up off the cardboard. Pluck each rubber band over the hole in the cardboard.

What sounds can you make? Do different rubber bands make different sounds? Use your fingers to stretch the rubber bands tight over the hole. Does the sound change?

See Vibrations

For this experiment you will need:
- a metal mixing bowl
- plastic wrap
- salt
- things you can use to make noise

Place the plastic wrap over the bowl and pull it tight on all sides. Sprinkle a thin layer of salt across the plastic wrap.

Now, make some noise! Drum on the side of the bowl (not on the plastic) with your fingers or a spoon. Bang two metal objects together. Clap your hands.

Observe the salt. What sounds cause the salt to jump? What sounds have little or no effect?

High Squeaks, Low Rumbles

The pitch of sound an animal can make depends on the length of its vocal cords. Animals with large heads have long vocal cords and animals with small heads have short vocal cords. A bat has a small head. It has short vocal cords small enough to fit in its tiny throat. A bat's vocal cords are so small they can only vibrate quickly. Bats make only high-pitched sounds.

Bats are active at night (nocturnal). Bats are not blind, but when they hunt for insects in the dark, they rely on their sense of sound more than their sense of sight. As a bat flies, it makes a series of squeaks. The sound waves bounce off of nearby objects like trees, rocks, and insects. The bat's large ears turn to catch the echoes. The sounds that bounce back tell the bat about its surroundings. This process is called **echolocation**.

An elephant has a large head. That means it also has a large throat and long vocal cords. They can vibrate slowly and make low-pitched sounds. Elephants can also make high-pitched sounds by shortening their vocal cords with the muscles in their larynx. Long vocal cords let elephants make a wide range of sounds.

Elephants live in herds. They have more than 70 sounds they use to communicate with other elephants. They can scream, roar, snort, rumble, squeal, cry, trumpet and groan. Just like people have different voices, each elephant has its own rumble. This helps the herd recognize each other from a distance. The rumbles are very loud, but too low-pitched for humans to hear. An elephant's rumble can carry for miles.

Predator or Prey Sorting

A **predator** is an animal that hunts other animals. **Prey** is an animal that is hunted. Some animals are both predator and prey.

Many predators quietly sneak up on the animals they are hunting. Some predators, like bats, use sounds to help them hunt prey.

Some prey animals make noise to scare off a predator or to warn other animals of danger. Others hide and stay quiet, hoping the predator won't notice them.

Sort the animals (below in **bold**) into predator, prey, or both. Answers are below.

1. A **python** slithers toward his next meal without making a sound. He wraps around a young monkey and squeezes tight before beginning to eat.

2. A **lioness** creeps silently through the long grass. She sneaks up on a gazelle and pounces.

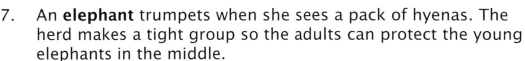

3. A **yellow-winged bat** squeaks in the quiet, night air. The echo tells her a tasty mosquito is nearby.

4. A **zebra** sees a leopard lurking in the grass. He brays and stomps his feet to warn the rest of his herd.

5. A **spiny mouse** squeals in fear when the hungry owl swoops down to grab her.

6. A **milky eagle owl**'s soft feathers don't make a sound as she moves her wings. She sees a mongoose and dives to snatch it off the ground.

7. An **elephant** trumpets when she sees a pack of hyenas. The herd makes a tight group so the adults can protect the young elephants in the middle.

8. A troop of **baboons** is hunting a gazelle when one sees a lioness on the prowl. The baboon gives a loud alarm. The rest of the troop hears the warning and they scurry up a tree to safety.

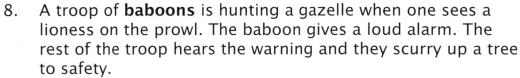

9. A **wildebeest** does not see the lion, but she hears a baboon call that one is nearby. She stomps her feet and starts to run. The rest of the herd follows her away from the hunting lion.

Predator: python, lioness, yellow-winged bat, and milky eagle owl
Prey: zebra, spiny mouse, elephant, and wildebeest
Both predator and prey: baboon

To Lou who makes it all possible—TCJ
To my parents for helping me love both art and science.—PS
Thanks to Stacy Graison, Vice President of Education at Zoo Atlanta, for reviewing the accuracy of the information in this book.

Library of Congress Cataloging-in-Publication Data

Jennings, Terry Catasús, author.
  Sounds of the savanna / by Terry Catasús Jennings ; illustrated by Phyllis Saroff.
      pages cm
  Summary: "From the first light of dawn until the sun sets at night, the savanna is alive with noise. A lion roars in the early morning, a young baboon shrieks at noon, and a young mouse squeals at dusk. What are the animals saying and why? Animals communicate in many ways; explore the thriving African savanna as its inhabitants "talk" to one another throughout the course of a day"-- Provided by publisher.
  Audience: Ages 4-8.
  Includes bibliographical references.
  ISBN 978-1-62855-632-2 (english hardcover) -- ISBN 978-1-62855-637-7 (english pbk.) -- ISBN 978-1-62855-647-6 (english downloadable ebook) -- ISBN 978-1-62855-657-5 (english interactive dual-language ebook) -- ISBN 978-1-62855-642-1 (spanish pbk.) -- ISBN 978-1-62855-652-0 (spanish downloadable ebook) -- ISBN 978-1-62855-662-9 (spanish interactive dual-language ebook) 1. Savanna animals--Juvenile literature. 2. Animal communication--Juvenile literature. 3. Sound--Juvenile literature. 4. Sound-waves--Juvenile literature. I. Saroff, Phyllis V., illustrator. II. Title.
  QL115.3.J46 2015
  591.59--dc23
                                    2015009000

Translated into Spanish: **Sonidos en la sabana**

Lexile® Level: AD 560L
key phrases for educators: Africa, EE (Environmental Education), food web, sound, predator/prey, communication, habitat: savanna/grassland

Bibliography:

Cawthon Lang KA. 2006 January 3. Primate Factsheets: Vervet (Chlorocebus) Behavior . <http://pin.primate.wisc.edu/factsheets/entry/vervet/behav>. Accessed 2013 November 18.
Cormier, Zoe. "African spiny mice can regrow lost skin." Nature. 26 September 2012. Accessed 2013 November 18. < http://www.nature.com/news/african-spiny-mice-can-regrow-lost-skin-1.11488>.
Fenton, M.B., Bats. Checkmark Books, 1992
Giancoli, Douglas C. Physics, Principles with Applications, Fifth Edition. New Jersey: Prentice Hall, 1998.
Kaufman, Rachel. "Zebra Stripes Evolved to Repel Bloodsuckers?" National Geographic. Published February 9, 2012. Accessed October 21, 2014.
 "The Larynx." UCLA. Accessed 2013 November 18. <http://www.linguistics.ucla.edu/people/ladefoge/manual%20files/chapter8.pdf>.

Manufactured in China, June 2015
This product conforms to CPSIA 2008
First Printing

Arbordale Publishing
Mt. Pleasant, SC 29464
www.ArbordalePublishing.com